POLISH COOKING

Food Photography by Peter Barry
All other photography by Chris Niedenthal
Recipes styled by Helen Burdett
Designed by Alison Jewell
Edited by Jillian Stewart

CLB 2664
© 1991 Colour Library Books Ltd., Godalming, Surrey, England.
All rights reserved.
This 1991 edition published by Crescent Books,
distributed by Outlet Book Company Inc., a Random House Company,
225 Park Avenue South, New York, New York 10003.
Color separations by Scantrans Pte Ltd, Singapore.
Printed and bound in Singapore.
ISBN 0 517 06147 3
8 7 6 5 4 3 2 1

POLISH COOKING

JUDITH FERGUSON

CRESCENT BOOKS
NEW YORK

INTRODUCTION

Polish cooking is country-style cooking and always has been. Warming stews, soups and meat dishes have long been the order of the day. This is not to say that there are no sophisticated dishes in the repertoire, but the nature of the people and the traditional crops dictate a hearty cuisine.

Poland lies in the heart of Europe, a location perfect for growing the cereal grains known as "kashas" which figure so importantly in early traditional recipes. A typical Polish pantry always contained certain staples that any self-respecting cook required. The country people were nothing if not self-sufficient. Indeed they had to be because harsh winters and long distances made traveling treacherous.

While the cuisine was traditional it was not without some foreign influence. Kings and princes often married noblewomen from other countries who had their own ideas on food and brought them, and indeed sometimes their cooks as well, to their new home. A young Italian princess who married into the Polish royal family in the sixteenth century found she was homesick for some traditional food so introduced tomatoes and pasta to the Poles.

Quantities of wheat and rye flours for making cakes, breads, pastries and dumplings were in good supply. Cereal grains or "kashas" were considered essential. Buckwheat was the most prized and served as a basis for both desserts and savory dishes.

When fresh mushrooms were plentiful, cooks pickled or dried them to use later. Fresh cabbages were shredded, covered with salt and weighted down to make sauerkraut. Cucumbers, fresh in summer, were made into salads with sour cream or sweet-sour vinegar dressings. Fruit such as apples, cherries and plums were dried or bottled to use later in the year for desserts and to serve with meat and game. The fruit also went into preserves, jams and liqueurs. Honey was kept in store to add to desserts and savory dishes such as noodles with poppy seeds. It was also used to make mead, a sweet, warming and very alcoholic drink.

Out in the farmyard, chickens and turkeys scratched for food, so fresh poultry was always available for roasting and adding to soups and stews. Once or twice a year a butcher would travel around to all the estates to kill a pig. Not a bit of it was wasted, and one pig produced sausages and blood puddings as well as hams and bacon. The hunting season meant variety, with partridge, pheasant, duck, rabbit, venison and wild boar all finding their way onto the table.

Fish from the rivers and lakes was served more often than salt water fish. Carp and pike were especially liked, so much so, that carp took pride of place on the table at Christmas Eve dinner. In the American Mid-West, the recipe for stuffed pike owes its origins to Poland. Herring was one fish from the sea that did find favor. It was fried, salted or pickled and served in a variety of ways. One of the nicest was herring spread, eaten on rye bread.

Polish food is made up of all of these good things, yet it is often overlooked and thought to be uninteresting. A taste of Polish cooking will soon convert a whole new generation to the delights of this most heartwarming cuisine.

Right: Poland has a rich folk heritage which is still much in evidence today.

Spring Vegetable Soup

Preparation Time: 10 minutes **Cooking Time:** 35 minutes **Serves:** 4-6

An enticing soup which can be adapted to incorporate your own favorite vegetables.

Ingredients

1 small head of cauliflower
3 carrots, peeled
2 kohlrabi, peeled
2 potatoes, peeled
2 tbsps butter or margarine
1 onion, peeled and chopped

6 cups chicken bouillon
1 cup cut green beans
1 tbsp chopped parsley
1 tsp chopped dill
Pinch of salt and pepper

Cut the cauliflower into small flowerets. Cut the carrots, kohlrabi and potatoes into one inch pieces. Melt the butter or margarine and cook the vegetables and the onion for a few minutes. Pour on the bouillon and bring to the boil, then simmer about 15 minutes. Add the green beans, parsley and dill and simmer a further 15 minutes or until vegetables are tender. Add salt and pepper to taste.

Much of Poland's agriculture is still dependant on old-fashioned methods and the help of the whole family.

Stuffed Eggs

Preparation Time: 20 minutes **Cooking Time:** 12-13 minutes **Serves:** 4

An inexpensive appetizer, these can also be a snack or canapé. The filling is delicious cold, too, so they are perfect for summer parties and picnics.

Ingredients
4 eggs
8oz cooked ham, ground
4 tbsps grated mild cheese
4 tbsps sour cream
2 tsps mustard

Pinch salt and pepper
2 tsps chopped fresh dill or chives
Dry breadcrumbs
Melted butter

Using a pin or egg pricker, make a small hole in the larger end of each egg to prevent the shell from cracking. Lower the eggs gently into boiling water. As the eggs come back to the boil, roll them around the pan with a spoon for about 2-3 minutes. This will help set yolk in the middle of the whites. Allow the eggs to cook 9-10 minutes after the water re-boils. Drain and place the eggs under cold running water. Allow to cool completely and leave in the cold water until ready to peel.

Peel the eggs, cut them in half lengthwise and remove the yolks. Combine yolks and all the remaining ingredients, except the breadcrumbs and melted butter, and mix well. Pipe or spoon the mixture into each egg white and mound the top, smoothing with a small knife. Sprinkle on the breadcrumbs, covering the filling and the edge of the whites completely. Place the eggs in a heatproof dish and drizzle with melted butter. Place under a preheated broiler for about 3 minutes, or until crisp and golden brown on top.

Thirteenth-century Malbork Castle in northern Poland is the largest Gothic fortress in Europe.

Spring Salad

Preparation Time: 20 minutes   **Serves:** 6

Don't save this salad just for spring – the ingredients are available all year round. Try it as a spread for sandwiches or a topping for canapés, too.

Ingredients

12-14oz cottage cheese
1 carrot, coarsely grated
8 radishes, coarsely grated
2 green onions, thinly sliced
Pinch salt and pepper

1 tsp chopped fresh dill or marjoram
½ cup sour cream or thick yogurt
Lettuce leaves (red oak leaf lettuce, curly endive or radicchio)

If cottage cheese is very liquid, pour into a fine strainer and leave to stand for about 15-20 minutes for some of the liquid to drain away. Alternatively, cut down on the amount of sour cream. Peel the carrot and shred using the coarse side of the grater or the coarse shredding blade in a food processor. Make sure the carrot is shredded into short strips. Shred the radishes with the grater and cut the onion into thin rounds with a large, sharp knife. Mix all the ingredients together, except the lettuce leaves, and chill for about 20 minutes to blend all the flavors.

To serve: place lettuce leaves on individual plates and mound the cottage cheese salad mixture on top. If desired, sprinkle with more chopped fresh dill.

Finely chopped red or green pepper or cucumber can be added to the salad. If using cucumber, grate and sprinkle with salt. Leave to stand for 30 minutes, rinse and pat dry.

Religious celebrations in Lowicz bring followers of all age groups together.

Easter Soup

Preparation Time: overnight **Cooking Time:** 65 minutes **Serves:** 4-6

Don't reserve this soup just for Easter, it's delicious all year round.

Ingredients

2 cups oatmeal
2 cups warm water
1 tbsp wine vinegar
1 tsp caraway seeds
1½lbs kielbasa
1½ quarts water

1 tbsp horseradish
1 tsp brown sugar
¼ tsp salt
⅛ tsp pepper
2 hard-cooked eggs
2 potatoes, cooked and sliced

Combine oatmeal, water, vinegar and caraway seeds in a bowl. Leave overnight to soak, then strain the liquid and reserve it. Cook the kielbasa in the water for one hour. Remove sausage and skim the fat from the surface of the cooking liquid. Combine sausage cooking liquid with strained oatmeal liquid and add horseradish, brown sugar, salt and pepper. Slice kielbasa, add it to the liquid and simmer for five minutes. Slice the hard-cooked eggs and arrange in soup bowls with the sliced potatoes. Spoon over the soup.

The castle at Lublin. The town developed on the old trade route linking Russia and central Europe.

Pig's Feet in Aspic

Preparation Time: 45 minutes **Cooking Time:** 4½ hours **Serves:** 6-8

Pigs were an important source of food in Poland and no part of them was wasted. The feet produce a stock which jells naturally.

Ingredients

1½ lbs pig's feet, cleaned
   and skinned
8oz pork or uncooked gammon,
   left whole
2 carrots, peeled
4 sticks celery
1 onion, quartered

2 bay leaves
5 black peppercorns
3 allspice berries
Pinch salt
6 tbsps white wine vinegar
2 egg whites
2 egg shells

Place the feet, pork, carrots, celery and onion into a large stockpot. Tie the bay leaves, peppercorns and allspice berries in a muslin bag and add to the pot. Pour in enough water to come 2 inches above the ingredients. Bring to the boil and then simmer, covered, for 2 hours. Add more water as necessary during cooking. Skim off any foam that collects on the surface during cooking. Add salt and vinegar and cook a further 2 hours and then strain, reserving about 3 pints of the liquid. Discard the muslin bag, remove pork and carrots and discard celery and onion. Take the meat off the feet and dice it along with the pork or gammon. Slice the carrot and set it aside. Strain the stock into a clean pan and add the egg whites and shells. Bring to the boil, whisking constantly until a thick foam forms on top. Allow the stock to boil up the sides of the pan, remove from the heat and allow to subside. Allow to boil up and subside twice more, but do not whisk. Strain into a clean bowl through a clean, scalded tea towel or piece of muslin. Let the foam fall into the towel and allow liquid to drain slowly through. Do not allow the crust to fall into the liquid. When the aspic is drained through, chill until syrupy.

Dampen a mold and pour in a thin layer of aspic. Chill in the refrigerator until firm. (If the aspic does not set when the first layer is chilled, add about 1 tbsp gelatine and re-heat.) Place slices of carrot in a decorative pattern on top and spoon on more aspic to set the carrot. Chill again until set. Mix the meat and the remaining aspic and fill up the mold. Chill until firm – at least 4 hours. Turn out and garnish the plate with parsley if desired.

Borsch with Pierozki

Preparation Time: 40 minutes **Cooking Time:** 1 hour **Serves:** 6-8

Borsch was served at both Christmas and Easter celebrations in Poland.

Dough
2 cups all-purpose flour
5oz butter or margarine

1 egg
1 tbsp yogurt or sour cream

Filling
Mushroom from the borsch
1 tbsp butter or margarine
1 small onion, finely chopped

1-2 tbsps fresh breadcrumbs
1 small egg
Salt and pepper

Borsch
1 celeriac
12 parsley stalks
4 carrots, peeled and chopped
3 leeks
1 onion, thinly sliced
3lbs uncooked beets
10 black peppercorns

3 whole allspice berries
1 bay leaf
2-3oz dried mushrooms
Juice of 1-2 lemons
$\frac{1}{3}$ cup dry red wine
1 clove garlic, crushed

Sift the flour with a pinch of salt into a large bowl. Cut the butter into small pieces and rub into the flour until the mixture resembles fine breadcrumbs. Mix egg and the yogurt or sour cream together and combine with the flour and butter to make a firm dough. Knead the dough together quickly, wrap well and chill for 30 minutes.

Peel the celeriac root and chop the root roughly. Chop the parsley stalks. Cut the leeks in half lengthwise, rinse well under cold running water and chop the leeks roughly. Place all the vegetables, except beets, in a large stockpot, add the black peppercorns, allspice berries and bay leaf and cover the vegetables with water. Cover and bring to the boil. Reduce the heat and allow to simmer, partially covered, for about 45 minutes. Place the dried mushrooms in a small saucepan and cover with 2 cups water. Cover, bring to the boil and simmer until the mushrooms soften. Strain and add liquid to vegetable stock. Chop the mushrooms finely.

For the filling, melt 1 tbsp butter in a small pan and add the onion and chopped mushrooms. Cook briskly to evaporate moisture, and blend in the breadcrumbs and egg and add seasoning. Add enough crumbs to help the mixture hold its shape. Set the filling aside to cool completely. Roll out dough thinly on a well-floured surface. Cut into circles about 3 inches in diameter. Fill with a spoonful of filling, seal the edges with water, fold over to seal and crimp with a fork. Bake on greased cookie sheets in a pre-heated 425°F oven for about 10-15 minutes, or until brown and crisp.

After the vegetable stock has cooked 45 minutes, add peeled, grated beets, lemon juice, red wine and garlic, and cook a further 15-20 minutes, or until a good red color. Strain and serve immediately with the pierozki.

Dumpling Soup

Preparation Time: 25 minutes **Cooking Time:** 1 hour 10 minutes **Serves:** 6-8

Dumplings with a variety of fillings are very popular in Poland. Use fewer dumplings per serving for an appetizer, more for a filling soup.

Ingredients
6 cups home-made beef stock

Chopped parsley

Filling
6oz ground beef or pork
1 tsp chopped fresh marjoram
Salt and pepper

1 small onion, grated or
  very finely chopped

Dough
2 cups all-purpose flour, sifted
Pinch salt
1-2 eggs

4 tbsps water

Combine all the filling ingredients, mixing very well. Prepare the dough by sifting the flour with a pinch of salt into a large bowl. Make a well in the center and add the eggs and water. Use only one egg if they are large. Using a wooden spoon beat the ingredients together, gradually incorporating flour from the outside until the dough becomes too stiff to beat. Knead the dough by hand until firm but elastic. Roll out the dough very thinly on a floured surface and cut into 3-inch rounds. Place a small spoonful of filling on each dough circle and brush the edges with water. Press the edges together to seal well, and crimp with a fork if desired.

Bring stock to the boil and add the dumplings. Cook about 10 minutes, or until all have floated to the surface. The dumplings may be cooked for the same length of time in water and dried and tossed with melted butter.

Add parsley to the soup, adjust the seasoning and serve in individual bowls or from a large tureen.

Chicken may be used in the dumpling filling in place of the beef or pork, and chicken stock substituted for beef stock.

Serve with sour cream and fresh dill or chives.

Mushrooms in Sour Cream

Preparation Time: 20 minutes **Cooking Time:** 5-7 minutes **Serves:** 4-6

This very old recipe originally called for freshly gathered forest mushrooms.

Ingredients
1lb button mushrooms, quartered
2 tbsps butter or margarine
6 green onions, thinly sliced
1 tbsp flour
1 tbsp lemon juice

2 tbsps chopped fresh dill or
  1 tbsp dried dill
Pinch salt and pepper
1/3 cup sour cream
Paprika

Rinse the mushrooms and pat dry. Trim the stalks level with the caps before quartering. Melt the butter in a sauté pan and add the mushrooms and onions. Sauté for about 1 minute and stir in the flour. Add the lemon juice and all the remaining ingredients except the sour cream and paprika and cook slowly for about 1 minute. Stir in the sour cream and adjust the seasoning. Heat through for about 1 minute. (Sour cream will curdle if boiled, although the addition of flour to the sauce will help to stabilize it somewhat.) Spoon into individual serving dishes or on top of buttered toast. Sprinkle with paprika and serve immediately.

Excellent as an appetizer or a side dish with meat, poultry or game. Prepare double quantity and serve with a salad and bread as a light lunch.

Horses are bred privately and sold at the many auctions around the country.

Beans and Carrots Polish Style

Preparation Time: 20 minutes **Cooking Time:** 20 minutes **Serves:** 4-6

Breadcrumbs browned in butter are often called a Polish sauce.

Ingredients

8oz green beans
8oz baby carrots with green tops
4 tbsps butter or margarine

4 tbsps dry breadcrumbs
½ tsp chopped, fresh dill or marjoram
Salt and pepper

Top and tail the beans. This is easier done in several large bunches. Leave some of the green tops on the carrots and peel them using a swivel vegetable peeler. Place the carrots in cold salted water, cover the pan and bring to the boil. Cook for 10-15 minutes after the water comes to the boil. The beans may be added during the last 5 minutes of cooking time or they may be cooked separately.

For the topping, melt the butter in a small saucepan and, when foaming, add the breadcrumbs, herbs and seasoning. Cook over low heat, stirring constantly until brown and crisp.

Drain the vegetables and mix them together. Sprinkle on the topping and serve. Frozen vegetables may be used instead, and the cooking times altered according to package directions.

Serve the vegetables as a side dish with meat, fish, poultry or game.

Rural life in Poland is simple, with farming still employing a large percentage of the workforce.

Beet Relish

Preparation Time: 5-10 minutes plus storing time

This tasty relish can be served with a whole range of dishes or on its own.

Ingredients

16oz can whole beets
¼ cup prepared horseradish
¼ cup sugar
¼ cup vinegar

¼ cup water
1 tbsp grated onion
1 tsp salt
⅛tsp pepper

Grate the beets or chop them finely in a food processor. Mix with the other ingredients and place in a covered container. Store in the refrigerator for at least one day before serving. Taste and add more sugar or vinegar as necessary. Serve with roast meats, boiled sausages or as an appetizer.

This colorful and vibrant example of Polish folk art depicts Adam and Eve in the Garden of Eden.

Noodles with Poppy Seeds and Raisins

Preparation Time: 15 minutes **Cooking Time:** 15-17 minutes **Serves:** 6

Christmas Eve dinner in Poland traditionally had up to 21 courses, of which this was but one!

Ingredients
Pinch salt
1 tbsp oil
8oz noodles or other pasta shapes
½ cup heavy cream

6 tbsps black poppy seed, ground
2 tbsps honey
6 tbsps raisins

Bring lots of water to the boil in a large saucepan with a pinch of salt. Add the oil and the noodles or other pasta shapes and bring back to the boil. Cook, uncovered, until tender, about 10-12 minutes. Drain and rinse the pasta under hot water. If using immediately, allow to drain dry. If not, place in a bowl of water to keep. Place the cream in a deep, heavy-based saucepan and bring almost to the boil. When the cream reaches the scalding point, mix in the poppy seeds, honey and raisins. Cook slowly for about 5 minutes. The mixture should become thick but still fall off a spoon easily. Use a food processor or spice mill to grind the poppy seeds. Toss the poppy seed mixture with the noodles and serve hot.

Serve as a course on its own in a Polish Christmas Eve dinner or ideal as a side dish to duck, pork or gammon.

Currants or golden raisins can be used instead of poppy seeds.

A life guard cabin watches over the sea on Poland's Baltic Coast.

Vegetable Salad

Preparation Time: 25-30 minutes   **Serves:** 4

Full of goodness and taste, this is the perfect summer salad.

Ingredients

1½lbs red potatoes
4 carrots, peeled and diced
1 small rutabaga, peeled and diced
2 dill pickles, choppped
8oz can navy beans, drained
1 cup frozen peas, cooked

4 hard-cooked eggs
1 cup mayonnaise
1 tsp spicy brown mustard
1 tbsp chopped dill
Paprika

Boil potatoes for 15 to 20 minutes. Drain thoroughly, peel and dice them. Cook the carrots and rutabaga in separate pans until tender. Combine vegetables with the pickles, beans and peas. Chop two of the eggs and add to the salad. Mix mayonnaise, mustard and dill and fold into the salad. Spoon into a bowl. Slice the remaining two eggs and arrange on the top of the salad. Sprinkle with paprika.

The impressive sixteenth-century market square and town hall in Zamosc is a striking example of Renaissance architecture.

Cauliflower Polish Style

Preparation Time: 20 minutes **Cooking Time:** 12-15 minutes **Serves** 4-6

A crunchy almond and golden fried breadcrumb topping brightens up a plain boiled cauliflower.

Ingredients

1 large head cauliflower	4 tbsps dry breadcrumbs
4 tbsps butter or margarine	2 hard-cooked eggs
4 tbsps finely chopped, blanched almonds	Chopped parsley and fresh dill

Remove the large coarse green leaves from the outside of the cauliflower. If desired, leave the fine pale green leaves attached. Trim the stem and wash the cauliflower well. Place the whole cauliflower in boiling water right side up. Add salt and bay leaf to the water and bring back to the boil. Cook the cauliflower for 12-15 minutes, or until just tender (do not overcook as cauliflower becomes watery very quickly). Melt the butter in a small frying pan and add the almonds. Cook slowly to brown. Stir in the breadcrumbs and cook about 1 minute or until crisp. Peel the eggs and cut them in half. Remove the yolks and cut the whites into thin strips. Press the yolks through a strainer.

When the cauliflower is cooked, drain it and place on serving dish. Spoon the breadcrumbs and almond topping over the cauliflower. Arrange the sliced egg white around the base of the cauliflower and sprinkle the egg yolks over the breadcrumb topping. Sprinkle over chopped parsley and dill. Serve immediately.

The beautiful Podhale region is dotted with picturesque villages.

Cucumber Salad

Preparation Time: 30 minutes   **Serves:** 6

In Polish this salad is known by the name *Mizeria* – quite a gloomy word for such a refreshing, delicious and versatile salad and side dish.

Ingredients

1 large cucumber
½ cup sour cream
2 tsps white wine vinegar

1 tsp sugar
1 tbsp chopped fresh dill
Salt and pepper

Wash the cucumber well. Trim off the thin ends of the cucumber. Using a cannelle knife or the prongs of a fork, score the skin of the cucumber in long strips. Cut the cucumber into thin slices and place in a colander. Sprinkle with salt and leave for 30 minutes. Place the colander in a bowl to collect the cucumber liquid. Rinse the cucumber well and pat dry. Mix the remaining ingredients together in a large bowl and toss with the cucumber slices.

Arrange the cucumber in a serving dish and serve chilled. Other chopped herbs may be used instead of, or in addition to, the dill.

The Palace of Nieborow is testimony to Poland's rich architectural heritage.

Polish-Style Lettuce Salad

Preparation Time: 20 minutes **Cooking Time:** 9-10 minutes **Serves:** 4-6

Polish style in this case means the use of sour cream and hard-cooked eggs in a dressing that really livens up plain lettuce salads.

Ingredients

1 head iceberg lettuce or 2 heads
   Webb or round lettuce
1 clove garlic
½ cup sour cream
Juice and grated rind of ½ lemon
½ tsp sugar
Salt and pepper
2 tsps chopped parsley
2 hard-cooked eggs

Break the lettuce into leaves and wash them well. Dry on paper towels or on a clean tea towel. Peel the clove of garlic and crush it with the side of a large knife. Rub the clove of garlic on the inside of a salad bowl.

Tear the lettuce into bite-sized pieces and place in the salad bowl. Mix together the remaining ingredients, except the hard-cooked eggs, and pour over the lettuce. Cut the hard-cooked eggs in half, remove the yolks and chop the whites finely. Scatter the white over the top of the dressing.

Place the yolks in a small sieve and hold it over a bowl. Using the back of a spoon or your fingers, push the yolk through the holes in the sieve and sprinkle yolks over the salad. Serve immediately.

Variation: add other ingredients such as sliced cucumber, grated carrot or diced peppers to the salad.

Although a great trading center, Gdansk is best known for its shipyard and as the birthplace of Solidarity.

Pickled Herring Spread

Preparation Time: 15 minutes

This unusual spread is easy to prepare and extremely tasty.

Ingredients
8oz jar marinated herring
2 hard-cooked eggs
¼ cup butter, softened

2 green onions, finely chopped
1 dill pickle, finely diced

Chop the herring coarsely and place in a food processor. Cut the eggs in half and add the yolks to the herring. Chop the egg whites finely and set them aside. Place the butter in the food processor with the herring and work the mixture until smooth. Mix in the chopped green onions, diced dill pickle and chopped egg white by hand. Chill and serve with sliced rye bread.

Northern Poland is littered with lakes and waterways which provide endless opportunities for sailors and fishermen.

Fried Carp

Cooking Time: 30-35 minutes   **Serves:** 4

Carp is a favorite fish in Poland and is prepared in numerous ways. This dish is popular on Christmas Eve.

Ingredients

1 cleaned, filleted carp weighing about 2-3lbs
Salt
Flour

1-2 eggs, lightly beaten
Dry breadcrumbs
Butter and oil for frying

Cabbage and Mushrooms Polish Style

1lb canned sauerkraut
2-3oz dried mushrooms
2 tbsps butter or margarine

1 onion, thinly sliced or finely chopped
1½ tbsps flour
Salt and pepper

Cut the cleaned and scaled carp into even-sized portions and sprinkle lightly with salt. Leave to stand for half an hour. Skin, if desired. Place the sauerkraut in a heavy-based saucepan and add 1 cup water. Bring to the boil and then allow to simmer until tender. Place the mushrooms in a separate pan and add enough water to cover. Cook over gentle heat until softened. Slice the mushrooms and reserve them and their cooking liquid. Melt the butter in a frying pan and, when foaming, add the onion. Cook in the butter until golden brown. Sprinkle over the flour and mix thoroughly. When the sauerkraut is tender, strain the cooking liquid over the butter mixture. Stir very well and bring to the boil. Cook until thickened and add to the sauerkraut, along with the sliced mushrooms and their liquid. Stir thoroughly and set aside to keep warm.

Dredge the carp lightly with flour, shaking off the excess. Coat with beaten egg using a pastry brush, or dip the pieces into the egg using two forks.

Place crumbs on wax paper and lift the sides to toss the crumbs over the fish, shaking off the excess. After coating several pieces of fish, breadcrumbs may clump together with the egg. Sift the breadcrumbs through a strainer and discard the eggy bits. Heat the butter and oil together in a large frying pan until very hot. Place in the fish and cook on both sides until golden brown – about 5 minutes per side. Make sure the oil and butter come half way up the sides of the fish. Drain fish on paper towels and serve immediately with the cabbage and mushrooms.

Polish-Style Herring

Preparation Time: 40 minutes **Cooking Time:** 30-40 minutes **Serves:** 4

Herring, prepared in any form, is a national favorite in Poland. These fish can be prepared well in advance and stored in their marinade.

Ingredients

4 even-sized herrings, cleaned
2 onions, thinly sliced
10 black peppercorns
5 whole allspice berries
2 bay leaves
1 lemon, sliced
Juice of 3 lemons

½ cup cream
½ tsp sugar
4 potatoes, peeled and sliced
Salt, pepper and caraway seed
6 tbsps vegetable oil
Lemon wedges and chopped
    parsley to garnish

Place fish open end downward on a chopping board. Press along the backbone with the heel of your hand to loosen the bone. Turn over and carefully pull out the main bone. Cut the fillets in half and skin them using a filleting knife, beginning at the tail end and working up to the head end using a sawing motion, with the knife at an angle to the skin. Layer the fillets in a deep casserole, placing onion slices, spices, bay leaves and lemon slices between each layer. Mix lemon juice and sugar together and pour over the fish. Place a sheet of wax paper directly over the top of the fish and cover with the casserole lid. Store in the refrigerator for 24 hours. Remove the fillets and strain the liquid. Mix 4 tbsps of the liquid with the cream and pour over the fillets to serve.

Layer the potatoes in an ovenproof serving dish and sprinkle salt, pepper, and caraway seeds in between each layer and on top. Spoon the oil over the top of the potatoes and bake, uncovered, in a preheated 400°F oven for about 30-40 minutes or until golden and cooked through. Serve with the herring. Garnish the dish with chopped parsley and lemon wedges.

The atmospheric Mazurian lake district was formed by the retreating ice sheets of the last ice age.

Stuffed Fish

Preparation Time: 20 minutes **Cooking Time:** 45 minutes **Serves:** 4-6

A whole baked fish makes an impressive main course for a dinner party. The stuffing makes the fish go further and with no bones it's easy to serve and eat.

Ingredients
2-3lbs whole fish such as carp, sea bass or salmon trout
2 tbsps melted butter

Stuffing
1 tbsp butter or margarine
1 small onion, finely chopped
4oz mushrooms, roughly
   chopped
1 hard-cooked egg, peeled and
   roughly chopped

¾cup fresh breadcrumbs,
   white or whole-wheat
Pinch salt and pepper
2 tsps chopped fresh dill
2 tsps chopped fresh parsley
Pinch nutmeg

Sauce
½cup sour cream
Pinch sugar
Grated rind and juice of ½lemon

Pinch salt and white pepper
Lemon slices and parsley sprigs
   to garnish

Ask the fishmonger to gut and bone the fish for you, leaving on the head and tail. Sprinkle the cavity of the fish with salt and pepper and set it aside while preparing the stuffing. Chop the onion finely. Melt the butter or margarine in a medium-sized saucepan and add the chopped onion and mushrooms. Cook briefly to soften the vegetables and set aside. Stir in the remaining stuffing ingredients. Spread the stuffing evenly into the cavity of the fish and place the fish in lightly buttered foil or in a large baking dish. Sprinkle the top with melted butter and bake in a preheated 350°F oven for about 40 minutes, basting frequently. If the fish begins to dry out too much on top, cover loosely with aluminum foil.

When the fish is cooked, combine the sauce ingredients and pour over the fish. Cook a further 5 minutes to heat the sauce, but do not allow it to bubble. Remove the fish to a serving dish and garnish with lemon and parsley.

Cabbage Rolls

Preparation Time: 30 minutes **Cooking Time:** 65-70 minutes **Serves:** 8-10

In Polish these are called *Golabki*, which translates as "little pigeons". They make a tasty, inexpensive supper dish, and you can improvise with different fillings.

Ingredients

1 head white cabbage or
   2 heads green cabbage
6oz rice
4 tbsps butter or margarine

1 large onion, chopped
10oz ground pork, veal or beef
Salt and pepper
1 egg

Sauce

2 tbsps butter or margarine
2 tbsps flour
2lbs canned tomatoes
1 clove garlic, crushed
½ cup chicken stock
1 tsp chopped fresh thyme

Pinch sugar
Salt and pepper
2 tbsps tomato paste
4 tbsps chopped parsley

Cut the core out of the cabbage completely. Place whole cabbage in boiling, salted water and cook for 15-20 minutes for green cabbage and 25-30 minutes for white cabbage. Remove and drain in a colander or on paper towels and leave to cool.

Cook the rice in boiling salted water for about 10 minutes or until almost tender. Drain and rinse under hot water to remove the starch. Leave to dry. Melt 4 tbsps butter or margarine in a large frying pan and cook the onion for about 3 minutes, or until slightly softened. Add the meat and cook slowly just until the meat loses its pink color. Break the meat up with a fork as it cooks. Add salt, pepper, rice and egg and set aside to cool. Separate the cabbage leaves and trim down the spines with a small, sharp knife. Place all the leaves out on a clean work surface and divide the filling evenly among all the leaves. To roll up, fold in the sides around the filling and roll up from the thick end to the thin end. Place all the cabbage rolls in a tightly-fitting casserole. It may be necessary to have two layers of rolls and possibly three. Pour water into the casserole to come about half way up the rolls. Cover the casserole tightly and cook in a preheated 375°F oven for 30 minutes.

To prepare the sauce, put 2 tbsps butter or margarine in a heavy-based pan and stir in the flour. Cook for 1-2 minutes and add all the remaining ingredients except the chopped parsley. Bring to the boil, stirring continuously. Partially cover the pan and cook for 20 minutes over low heat. Break up the tomatoes with a fork as the sauce cooks.

Check the level of liquid in the casserole. Pour away all but ½ cup. Pour on the tomato sauce and cook, uncovered, for a further 20 minutes, or until the cabbage is tender. Sprinkle with chopped parsley before serving.

Stuffed Roast Beef

Preparation Time: 30 minutes **Cooking Time:** 1 hour 15 minutes **Serves:** 6

The roasting is done on top of the stove instead of in the oven. This means a succulent piece of meat with a moist stuffing.

Ingredients
2 tbsps butter
2lb beef joint
Flour

1 cup beef stock
1 bay leaf
1 blade mace

Stuffing
2 tbsps butter or margarine
3 medium onions, peeled and
  finely chopped
3-4 slices bread, made into crumbs
Grated rind and juice of ½ lemon

2 tsps chopped parsley
1 tsp chopped thyme
1 egg
Pinch paprika
Salt and pepper

Melt the 2 tbsps butter in a large saucepan. Coat the meat with flour and brown the meat in the butter on all sides. Pour the stock into the casserole and add the bay leaf, blade mace and a pinch of pepper. Cover the pan and cook on top of the stove over low heat for about 45 minutes, turning the joint from time to time and adding more water or stock if necessary.

Remove the joint from the casserole and place it on a cutting board to stand for 10-15 minutes. Melt the remaining butter in a saucepan and add the chopped onions. Cook until the onions are tender, but not brown. Add the breadcrumbs and remaining stuffing ingredients, beating well to mix thoroughly. Slice the joint thinly, but without cutting completely through the meat. Spread an even amount of stuffing between each slice of meat and press the joint back into shape. Return the joint to the casserole for a further 35-40 minutes. When the meat is tender, remove it to a serving dish and boil the pan juices rapidly until of syrupy consistency. Pour some over the joint and serve the rest separately.

Fall brings a quiet beauty to the Polish countryside near Warsaw.

Breaded Veal Chops

Preparation Time: 10 minutes **Cooking Time:** 40 minutes **Serves:** 4

This traditional dish is the perfect mid-week meal.

Ingredients

4 rib veal chops	Fresh white breadcrumbs,
Flour	finely ground
¼ tsp salt	6 tbsps oil
⅛ tsp pepper	4 tbsps butter
¼ tsp paprika	1 cup heavy cream
2 eggs, beaten	2 tsps chopped parsley

Leave rib bones attached to the chops and pound meat to flatten slightly. Mix flour, salt, pepper and paprika and coat chops, shaking off the excess. Dip chops in beaten eggs then in the breadcrumbs, pressing to coat evenly. Heat oil in a large frying pan and drop in butter. Cook chops over moderate heat until golden brown, about 30 minutes, turning frequently. Remove and keep warm in a low oven. Drain all but one tablespoon of the fat from the pan. Add 1 tablespoon flour and cook a few seconds. Pour in cream and stir until smooth. Bring to the boil, then simmer to thicken. Add parsley and pour sauce over the chops. Sprinkle with more paprika and serve with noodles.

Winter in the Tatra Mountains is a beautiful, if cold, time of year.

Hunter's Stew

Preparation Time: 25 minutes **Cooking Time:** 1 hour 25 minutes **Serves:** 8

The tradition of this stew – *Bigos* in Polish – goes back centuries. The ingredients were kept in good supply in larders, and the stew was taken on long road journeys and eaten on feast days.

Ingredients

4 tbsps oil
¾lb stewing steak, pork or
    venison cut in 2-inch pieces
1 onion
2 cloves garlic, crushed
4 tbsps flour
2 tbsps mild paprika
4 cups light stock
4oz smoked ham, cut in
    2-inch pieces
4oz smoked sausage, cut in
    2-inch pieces
1 tsp marjoram

1 tsp chopped thyme
1 tsp chopped parsley
Salt and pepper
Pinch cayenne pepper (optional)
2 tbsps tomato paste
1 head white cabbage, chopped
2 apples, cored and chopped
2 carrots, thinly sliced
8 pitted prunes, roughly chopped
3 tomatoes, peeled and roughly
    chopped
⅓ cup red wine or Madeira
Pinch sugar (optional)

Heat the oil in a large, flameproof casserole. Slice onion thickly and add with the garlic and cook 2-3 minutes. Remove and set aside. Add the meat in four small batches, cooking over high heat to brown. When all the meat is browned, return it to the casserole with the onion and garlic. Sprinkle over the flour and cook until light brown. Add paprika and cook 1-2 minutes, stirring constantly. Pour on the stock gradually and bring to the boil. Turn down the heat to simmering and add the smoked meats, herbs, salt, pepper, cayenne and tomato paste. Stir well, cover and cook over low heat for 45 minutes. Stir occasionally and add more liquid if necessary during cooking. When the meat is almost tender, add cabbage, apples, carrots and prunes. Cook a further 20 minutes. Add the tomatoes, wine or Madeira and a pinch of sugar, if desired. Cook a further 10 minutes, adjust the seasoning and serve immediately.

Filled Beef Rolls

Preparation Time: 25 minutes **Cooking Time:** 1 hour **Serves:** 4

Zrazy, thin slices of tender beef, go back to the 14th century in Polish cuisine. There are different kinds of *zrazy* and many different stuffings for the rolled variety.

Ingredients

8 thin frying steaks, trimmed
2 dill pickles, cut in thin strips
4oz cooked ham steak,
    cut in thin strips
2 green onions, shredded
Mustard
4 tbsps oil

2 tbsps flour
1 cup beef stock
4 tbsps white wine
1 tbsp tomato paste
Salt and pepper
4 tbsps sour cream or thick yogurt
Chopped parsley

Place each steak between two sheets of damp wax paper and bat out with a meat mallet or rolling pin to flatten. Cut the dill pickles, ham and green onion into even-sized lengths. Spread the meat thinly with the mustard and divide the dill pickles, ham and onions among all the slices. Fold in the sides of the meat about ½ inch. Roll the meat around the filling and secure with wooden picks or tie with fine string.

Heat the oil in a large sauté pan and when hot, brown the beef rolls. It may be necessary to brown them in two batches. Remove the meat and set aside. Add the flour to the pan and allow to cook until light brown. Gradually stir in the stock an add the wine, tomato paste, salt and pepper. Bring to the boil and allow to simmer for one minute. Return the beef rolls to the pan and spoon over some of the sauce. Cover and cook over low heat for 45 minutes to 1 hour. Add more liquid as necessary during cooking.

When the beef rolls are cooked, transfer them to a serving dish and remove the wooden picks or string. Spoon over the sauce and top with sour cream and chopped parsley to serve.

Variation: other filling ingredients such as mushrooms, sauerkraut, herbs and breadcrumbs or horseradish and breadcrumbs bound with egg may be used.

Excellent served with pasta, rice or mashed potatoes.

Roast Pork in Wild Game Style

Cooking Time: 1 hour 10 minutes   **Serves:** 6-8

The love of game is part of Polish culinary history, so even meat from domestic animals was often given the same treatment.

Ingredients

3lb boneless pork roast
Paprika
4 tbsps lard or dripping

¾ cup sour cream or thick yogurt
1 tsp flour
1 tbsp chopped fresh dill

Marinade

1 carrot, finely chopped
2 celery sticks, finely chopped
1 bay leaf
5 black peppercorns
5 allspice berries

2 sprigs thyme
10 juniper berries, slightly crushed
2 onions, sliced
½ cup dry white wine
Juice and grated rind of 1 lemon

Beet accompaniment

4 tbsps butter or margarine
2 tbsps flour
1 onion, finely chopped
1 clove garlic, crushed
½ cup chicken or vegetable stock

2lbs cooked beet, peeled and grated
   or cut into small dice
White wine vinegar
Sugar, salt and pepper

First combine the marinade ingredients in a small saucepan and bring to the boil. Allow to cool. Place the pork in a casserole dish or bowl and pour over the marinade. Cover and refrigerate for two days, turning the meat frequently. Remove the meat from the marinade and wipe it dry with paper towels. Reserve the marinade. Heat the lard or dripping in a roasting pan. Sprinkle the fat side of the pork with paprika, and brown the pork on all sides in the hot fat. Pour over marinade after one hour's cooking. Cook, uncovered, in a preheated 375°F oven for 2 hours and 15 minutes. Baste frequently with the pan juices. Remove the pork from the pan and set aside. Skim any fat from the surface of the sauce and strain the vegetables and meat juices into a saucepan. Mix the sour cream, flour, and dill together and add to the pan. Bring just to the boil, turn down the heat and allow to simmer for 1-2 minutes. Grate the beet or cut it into small dice. Melt the butter in a heavy-based saucepan and add the flour and onion. Stir well and cook over moderate heat until light brown. Add the garlic and stir in the stock gradually. Bring to the boil, add beet, vinegar, sugar, salt and pepper to taste, and cook for ten minutes over moderate heat. Stir occasionally to prevent sticking.

Make the beet accompaniment just before serving. To serve, slice the pork and pour over the sauce. Serve with the beet.

Roast Pork with Caraway Seeds

Preparation Time: 35-40 minutes **Cooking Time:** 1 hour 15 minutes **Serves:** 6

In old Poland, pork was the most popular meat because there was such an abundance of wild boar in the forests.

Ingredients

2lb pork roast
Salt
Marjoram
2 tsps caraway seed

1½ tbsps lard or oil
2 onions, sliced
1 cup stock

Potato Kopythka

2lbs potatoes, peeled and cooked
1 large egg

1lb all-purpose flour
Salt

Remove the crackling, leaving most of the fat on the joint. Place crackling in a shallow pan, brush lightly with oil and sprinkle with salt. Score the fat of the joint in a chequerboard pattern. Sprinkle with salt, a pinch of marjoram and the caraway seeds at least one hour before cooking. Heat the lard in a roasting pan and brown the meat, fat side down first. Cook on all sides and then turn over fat side down again. Add the onions and the stock. Roast in a preheated 425°F oven for 30 minutes. Turn over and continue roasting for 45 minutes or until the juices run clear, basting frequently with the cooking liquid. Cook the crackling at the same time, turning it over halfway through the cooking time.

Meanwhile, cook the potatoes, drain them, place back in the pan and toss over high heat to dry completely. Push them through a sieve into a large bowl. Beat in the egg and gradually add the flour with a good pinch of salt. Turn the mixture out onto a floured surface and knead until a smooth dough forms. Divide the dough into 4-6 pieces and roll each into a sausage shape about 1-inch thick. Cut into diagonal pieces about 2-inches long. Drop the dough pieces into boiling salted water and cook until they float to the surface and are slightly firm. Drain the dumplings and keep warm. Carve the joint into slices or bring to the table whole. Skim the fat from the surface of the pan juices and reduce them slightly if necessary by boiling over high heat. Pour around the meat to serve. Crumble the crackling over the Kopytka and serve with pork.

Roast Pigeon with Juniper Sauce

Cooking Time: 1 hour 10 minutes   **Serves:** 2

This sauce goes as well with venison as it does with game birds.

Ingredients
2 pigeons, dressed
4oz chicken liver pâté

1 tbsp brandy
6 strips bacon

Sauce
2oz smoked bacon, chopped
1 onion, finely chopped
½ carrot, finely chopped
1 stick celery, finely chopped
1 tbsp juniper berries

2 tbsps flour
1 cup stock
½ cup white wine
1 tsp tomato paste (optional)
Salt and pepper

Pluck any pin feathers from the pigeons with tweezers or singe them over a gas flame. Mix pâté and brandy together and spread on the insides of each pigeon. Tie the 6 strips bacon on the pigeons to cover the breast and roast them in a preheated 400°F oven for 35-40 minutes.

Meanwhile, place chopped bacon in a heavy-based saucepan over low heat. Cook slowly to render the fat. Add the vegetables and juniper berries and cook until the vegetables begin to brown lightly. Add the flour and cook until golden brown (do not allow the vegetables to become too brown before adding the flour as the sauce will taste bitter). Pour on stock gradually, stirring continuously. Bring to the boil and reduce the heat to simmer. Partially cover the pan and cook slowly for about 20-25 minutes. Add more stock or water as necessary.

Skim the fat from the roasting pan and discard it. Add pan juices to the sauce and pour in the juices from the cavity of each pigeon. Strain the sauce into a clean pan and add the wine and tomato paste, if using.

Bring to the boil for about 3 minutes to reduce slightly. Season with salt and pepper and serve with the pigeons.

Accompany with noodles or potatoes. Serving and eating are easier if the pigeons are cut in half first.

Chicken Polish Style

Preparation Time: 20 minutes **Cooking Time:** 45 minutes **Serves:** 4

Choose small, young chickens for a truly Polish style dish. A dried white roll was originally used for stuffing, but breadcrumbs are easier.

Ingredients

2 chickens, weighing
   approximately 2lbs each
2 chicken livers
1 tbsp butter or margarine
6 slices bread, made into crumbs

2 tsps chopped parsley
1 tsp chopped dill
1 egg
Salt and pepper
½ cup chicken stock

Remove the fat from just inside the cavities of the chickens and discard it. Melt the butter in a small frying pan. Pick over the chicken livers and cut away any discolored portions. Add chicken livers to the butter and cook until just brown. Chop and set aside. Combine the breadcrumbs, egg, herbs, salt and pepper and mix well. Chopped mushrooms or onions may be added to the stuffing, if desired. Mix in the chopped chicken livers. Stuff the cavities of the chickens and sew up the openings with fine thread using a trussing needle. Tie the legs together. Place the chickens in a roasting pan and spread the breasts and legs lightly with more butter. Pour the stock around the chickens and roast in a preheated 375°F oven for about 40-45 minutes. Baste frequently with the pan juices during roasting. To check if the chickens are done, pierce the thickest part of the thigh with a skewer or small, sharp knife. If the juices run clear, the chickens are ready. If the juices are pink, return to the oven for another 5-10 minutes.

When the chickens are done, remove them from the roasting pan, remove the strings and keep them warm. Skim any fat from the surface of the pan juices. If a lot of liquid has accumulated, pour into a small saucepan and reduce over high heat. Pour the juices over the chicken to serve.

Serve with a cucumber salad or a Polish style lettuce salad and new potatoes tossed with butter and dill.

Clouds gather over the sand dunes at Debki beach near Gdansk.

Duck in Caper Sauce

Preparation Time: 20 minutes **Cooking Time:** 1 hour **Serves:** 2-3

A sweet-sour sauce with the tang of capers is a perfect accompaniment to a rich meat such as duck.

Ingredients

4½ lbs whole duck,
   giblets removed
1 clove garlic, crushed
Salt and pepper
1 tbsp oil
3 tbsps butter or margarine
1 cup chicken stock

4 tbsps sugar
½ cup water
1 tbsp vinegar or lemon juice
6 tbsps capers
4 tsps cornstarch mixed with
   2 tbsps water

Rub the cavity of the duck with the crushed garlic and sprinkle in salt and pepper. Leave to stand 1-2 hours but do not refrigerate. Heat the oil in a heavy frying pan or roasting pan and when hot add the butter or margarine. Prick the duck skin all over with a sharp fork and brown the duck on all sides in the butter and oil. Transfer the duck to a saucepan or flameproof casserole. Pour over the stock, cover and simmer over medium heat for about 1 hour 40 minutes, or until the duck is tender.

Meanwhile, heat the water and sugar together slowly in a small, heavy-based saucepan until the sugar dissolves. Once the sugar is dissolved, turn up the heat and allow the syrup to boil rapidly until it caramelizes. Remove from the heat and pour in the vinegar or lemon juice. It will splutter. Add several spoonfuls of the cooking liquid from the duck and set the caramel over medium heat. Allow mixture to come to the boil, stirring constantly.

When the duck is tender, remove it to a heated serving dish. Skim off the fat from the cooking liquid and discard. Mix the water and cornstarch together and add several spoonfuls of the duck cooking liquid. Return to the rest of the liquid and bring to the boil. Add the capers and stir over high heat until the sauce clears and thickens. Add the caramel and stir until the sauce is thick. Cut the duck into portions or serve whole and spoon over some of the sauce. Serve the rest of the sauce separately.

Roast Quail

Preparation Time: 20-25 minutes **Cooking Time:** 20 minutes **Serves:** 4

Quail are delicate, very elegant birds that are perfect as a dinner party dish. They are also easy to prepare and quick to cook – a bonus when entertaining.

Ingredients

8 dressed quail
8 thin slices pork fat or
   8 strips bacon
Fresh sage leaves

4oz butter
8 slices white bread, crusts removed
Whole cranberry sauce or blueberry
   preserves with the juice of ½ lemon

Remove any pin feathers from the birds and wash them under cold running water. Dry thoroughly inside and out. Salt lightly inside and place a fresh sage leaf inside each quail. Tie the pork fat or bacon strips around each bird. Melt the butter over a low heat and brush over each bird before placing them in a preheated 400°F oven for about 20-25 minutes. Baste the quail from time to time with the melted butter and the pan juices. Put the remaining butter in a large frying pan and place over fairly high heat. When hot, add slices of bread which have been cut to a size to fit the quail. Brown them on both sides in the butter and remove to paper towels to drain. When the quail are cooked, remove the threads and take off the bacon or pork fat, if desired. The fat or bacon may be served with the quail. Place each quail on a piece of fried bread and serve with whole cranberry sauce or the blueberry preserves mixed with lemon juice. Spoon some of the pan juices over each quail before serving.

A patchwork of fields in the Tatra foothills in Southern Poland.

Sweet Pierozki

Preparation Time: 50-60 minutes **Cooking Time:** 15 minutes **Serves:** 8

In Polish cuisine, dumplings can be sweet as well as savory. Surprisingly, these are often eaten as a side dish to meat or as a main dish by themselves.

Ingredients
Dough
Full quantity dough recipe for
  Borsch with Pierozki

Oil for frying

Cheese Filling
8oz dry cottage cheese
1 egg yolk
2 tbsps sugar

2 tsps finely chopped
  candied orange peel
2 tbsps currants

Plum Filling
4-6 purple plums, halved,
  pitted and chopped
⅓ cup sugar

Sour cream
Grated nutmeg or cinnamon

Prepare the dough as for the Pierozki in the Borsch recipe. Roll out very thinly on a well-floured surface and cut into circles about 3 inches in diameter.

For the cheese filling, beat the cottage cheese, egg yolk and sugar together until smooth. Stir in the peel and the currants by hand.

Place a spoonful of the filling on half of the dough circles and moisten the edges with water. Fold over the top and seal the edges well, crimping with a fork if desired. On the remaining half of the dough circles, place on some of the chopped plums and sprinkle with sugar. Seal the edges as before.

To cook the Pierozki, drop a few at a time into boiling water. Simmer for 2-3 minutes or until they float to the top. Lift out of the water with a slotted spoon and drain on paper towels. When all the Pierozki are done, heat about 4 tbsps oil in a frying pan and cook the Pierozki over brisk heat for about 3-4 minutes, or until lightly browned on both sides. Place the Pierozki on a serving plate and top with sour cream sprinkled with nutmeg or cinnamon.

Variation: other fruit such as pitted cherries, apricots or peaches, pitted and chopped, may be used.

Pierozki can be cooked in advance and fried just before serving.

Polish-Style Doughnuts

Preparation Time: 40 minutes   **Cooking Time:** 5 minutes

Doughnuts are popular with all age groups and these are particularly tasty.

Ingredients
1 package active dry yeast
¾ cup warm water
⅓ cup butter or margarine
⅔ cup sugar
1 whole egg
3 egg yolks
1 tsp vanilla extract

1 tsp grated orange or
    lemon peel
¼ tsp salt
3½ cups all-purpose flour
Oil for deep frying
Confectioners' sugar (optional)

Dissolve yeast in warm water. Cream butter or margarine and sugar until light and fluffy. Beat in the whole egg, then egg yolks, one at a time. Add vanilla extract, grated peel, dissolved yeast and salt. Beat until well mixed. Stir in flour gradually, adding enough to make a stiff dough. Turn dough onto a floured surface. Knead until smooth and elastic – about 10 minutes.

Place dough in a greased bowl and cover. Leave in a warm place to rise until doubled in bulk. Turn dough out onto a lightly floured surface and knead again for a few minutes. Pat or roll out to ½-inch thickness. Cut out with a round doughnut cutter. Cover and leave to rise again until doubled in size. Heat oil to 375°F and fry the doughnuts 2 to 3 minutes, turning to brown both sides. Drain well on paper towels and sprinkle with confectioners' sugar, if desired.

The northern town of Torun is rich in architectural treasures.

Poppy Seed Cake

Preparation Time: 1 hour **Cooking Time:** 45-50 minutes **Makes:** 2 rolls

This is the Christmas version of an ever popular Polish cake. As a symbol of holiday generosity, more poppy seeds were used than in the everyday recipe.

Ingredients
Pastry Dough

6 cups all-purpose flour

¾ cup sugar

1½ sticks butter or margarine

2 eggs

⅓-½ cup milk

3 tbsps yeast

Pinch salt

Filling

8oz poppy seeds

1½ cups milk

⅓ cup butter or margarine

½ cup honey

4 tbsps ground walnuts

3oz raisins

2 tbsps finely chopped candied peel

2 eggs

½ cup sugar

⅓ cup brandy

To prepare the dough, cream the butter with the sugar until light and fluffy and gradually add the eggs, beating well in between each addition. Add a pinch of salt and heat the milk until lukewarm. Dissolve the yeast in the milk and add to the other ingredients. Sift in the flour and knead the dough until smooth and elastic. When kneading dough, be sure to stretch it well and work on a lightly-floured surface. If necessary, flour hands if the dough tends to stick. To test if the dough has been sufficiently kneaded, press lightly with two fingers. If the dough springs back fairly quickly, it is ready to leave to rise. Place the dough in a lightly greased bowl, cover with a cloth of lightly greased plastic wrap and leave for about 1 hour, or until doubled in bulk. Keep in a warm place. Bring the milk for the filling to the boil and mix with the poppy seeds. Cook over low heat for about 30 minutes, stirring frequently. Drain the poppy seed well and blend to a paste in a food processor or liquidizer. Melt the butter and add the honey, walnuts, raisins and peel. Add the poppy seeds and cook for about 15 minutes, stirring frequently over moderate heat. Beat the eggs with the sugar until light and fluffy and combine with the poppy seed mixture. Cook over gentle heat, stirring constantly to thicken. Add the brandy and set the filling aside.

When the dough has doubled in bulk, knock it back and knead for a further 2-5 minutes. Divide dough in half. Roll each half out thinly on a floured surface, shaping into rectangles. Spread the filling evenly over each piece and roll up as for a jelly roll. Roll up tightly, pressing the ends together to seal. Place on a lightly buttered baking sheet curving into a horse shoe. Bake in a preheated 375°F oven for 45-50 minutes, or until golden brown. Serve with or without icing.

Crullers

Preparation Time: 45 minutes **Cooking Time:** 20 minutes **Makes:** 36

These are crisp, light biscuits that are fried like fritters. They are best eaten on the day they are made and are lovely with coffee or tea.

Ingredients

2 egg yolks
1 whole egg
4 tbsps sugar
4 tbsps whipping cream

1¼ cups all-purpose flour
Pinch salt
Powdered sugar
Oil for deep frying

Beat yolks and whole egg together until thick and lemon colored – about 10 minutes. Add the sugar and beat well to dissolve. Sift the flour with a pinch of salt and whisk half of it into the egg mixture, alternating with the cream. Fold in the remaining flour. Leave to stand 30 minutes in a cool place.

Turn the dough out onto a well-floured surface and knead with floured hands. Dough will be sticky at first. Roll out until very thin with a well-floured rolling pin on a well-floured surface. Using a fluted pastry wheel, cut into strips about 3 x 1½ inches. Cut a slit in the lower half of each piece. Pull one end through the slit. Deep fry at 350°F until golden brown on both sides – about 3-4 minutes, cook a maximum of 6 crullers at a time. Drain on paper towels and sprinkle with powdered sugar before serving.

Serve as an accompaniment to fruit or ice cream, or serve with coffee or tea.

A religious festival in the town of Kadzidlo is a colorful affair for the participants.

Royal Mazurek

Preparation Time: 30 minutes **Cooking Time:** 20-30 minutes **Serves:** 8

Mazureks are flat pastry cakes and there are many different recipes for these. The dough needs careful handling, but the result is well worth the effort.

Ingredients

1½ sticks butter or margarine
4 tbsps sugar
6 tbsps blanched almonds, finely chopped
½ tsp grated lemon rind
2½ cups all-purpose flour
Yolks of 2 hard-cooked eggs, sieved
1 raw egg yolk
Pinch salt
Pinch cinnamon
Apricot and raspberry or cherry preserves
Powdered sugar

Cream the butter and the sugar together until light and fluffy. Stir in the almonds, lemon rind, flour and egg yolks by hand. Add the raw egg yolk and a pinch of salt and cinnamon, and mix all the ingredients into a smooth dough. This may be done in a food processor. Wrap well and leave in the refrigerator for about 1 hour. Roll out ⅔ of the dough and place on a baking sheet. If dough cracks, press back into place. Keep remaining ⅓ of the dough in the refrigerator. Roll out the remaining dough and cut into thin strips about ¼-inch thick. Arrange these strips on top of the dough in a lattice pattern and press the edges to seal. Brush the pastry with a mixture of 1 beaten egg with a pinch of salt. Bake in a preheated 375°F oven for about 20-30 minutes, or until light golden brown and crisp. Loosen the pastry from the baking sheet but do not remove until completely cool. Place the pastry on a serving plate and spoon some of the preserves into each of the open spaces of the lattice work. Alternate the two flavors of preserves. Sprinkle lightly with powdered sugar before serving.

Warsaw is situated at the site of an ancient crossing point on the Vistula River.

Saffron Babas

Preparation Time: 2 hours **Cooking Time:** 1 hour **Makes:** 2 cakes

This is a traditional Easter cake. Cooks spoke in whispers when these cakes were cooking since loud noise was believed to damage the delicate texture!

Ingredients

2½ cups all-purpose flour
1½ cups lukewarm milk
3 envelopes dry yeast
¾ cup sugar
8 egg yolks
4 egg whites
Rind of 1 lemon
3 tbsps brandy

Pinch saffron powder
7½ cups all-purpose flour
Pinch salt
1½ sticks melted butter,
    slightly cooled
1 cup golden raisins
2 tbsps candied peel

First prepare a batter with 2½ cups flour. Combine the milk and yeast and pour into a well in the center of the flour. Mix with a wooden spoon and cover the bowl. Leave in a warm place for about 1 hour, covered with a cloth or plastic wrap, until it doubles in bulk and the top becomes bubbly. Combine the sugar together with the egg yolks, egg whites, lemon rind, brandy and saffron. Mix with the yeast mixture and add the remaining flour and salt. Knead the dough by hand for about 30 minutes in the bowl or on a very well-floured surface. Place the dough back in the bowl and add the butter, raisins and peel. Knead the dough by hand until it is smooth and elastic and does not stick. Divide in two equal portions. Butter two 10-inch round cake pans very thickly and place in the dough, patting out evenly. Cover with lightly-oiled plastic wrap and put in a warm place to rise until it fills the pan. Bake in a preheated 400°F oven for about 60 minutes. Test with a metal skewer. If the skewer comes out clean when inserted into the center of the babas the cakes are done. Leave to cool in the pans for about 10-14 minutes and then remove to a cooling rack. Sprinkle with sugar or drizzle with icing.

Warsaw in the early spring. Much of the city was rebuilt after the Second World War.

Buckwheat and Raisin Pudding

Preparation Time: 20 minutes **Cooking Time:** 1 hour 25 minutes **Serves:** 6-8

Of all the cereals or *kashas* used in Polish cooking, buckwheat was the most highly prized.

Ingredients

3 cups milk
1 vanilla pod
6 tbsps butter or margarine
1 cup buckwheat
4 eggs, separated

¾ cup sugar
1-1¼ cups raisins
Grated rind of half a lemon
Red cherry preserves

Boil the milk with the vanilla pod in a large saucepan. Stir in 4 tbsps of the butter until melted. Reserve remaining butter. Pick over the buckwheat and add it to the milk, stirring well. Cook, uncovered, over low heat, stirring occasionally to prevent sticking.

When the mixture thickens, transfer it to an ovenproof dish with tight – fitting lid. Bake in a preheated 375°F oven for 45 minutes. Remove the vanilla pod and allow the mixture to cool slightly. Beat the egg yolks with the sugar until light and fluffy. Add lemon rind, mix with the buckwheat, and stir in the raisins. Whisk egg whites until stiff peaks form and fold into the buckwheat mixture. Smooth the top of the pudding and dot with the remaining butter. Bake a further 30 minutes at 375°F. Serve topped with cherry preserves and cream, if desired.

Churches such as the Orthodox Church at Bialowieza are central to Polish everyday life.